DAY BOOK

A dateless diary in an enchanting floral theme

READ ON
PUBLICATIONS
INCORPORATED

This edition published in 1996 by
READ ON
Publications Inc,
100 The East Mall, Unit 5
Toronto, Ontario M8Z 5X2, Canada
Phone: (416) 503-3444
Fax: (416) 503-9386

ISBN 1 85967 132 2

Produced by Anness Publishing Limited
Boundary Row Studios
1 Boundary Row
London SE1 8HP

Printed and bound in Singapore

Important Dates

January

February

March

April

May

June

July

August

September

October

November

December

JANUARY

Beneath every snowing
A thaw
And a growing
A greening and growing

Native American saying

1

2

3

4

5

6

7

The pleasing texture and sympathetic look of the terracotta pot complement the red roses and subdued green of the moss beautifully. Containers are often an integral part of an arrangement so should be selected with thought.

8

9

10

11

12

13

14

15

16

17

A pretty candle gift-pot
heralds the new year.

18

19

20

21

22

23

24

Sculptural arum lilies and aucuba 'Gold Dust' create an elegant and stately display, supported by comported willow. Arum lilies are so pure in colour and form that they need only the minimum of well-chosen foliage to support them.

25

26

27

28

29

30

31

The flowers of the gerbera are perfect for simple, bold, modern designs. This display isolates blooms in separate containers within an overall grouping. The impact is perpetuated in the water by the addition of food colouring.

FEBRUARY

One month is past, another is begun
Since merry bells rang out the dying year
And buds of rarest green began to peer
As if impatient for a warmer sun

Hartley Coleridge: 1 February 1842

1

5

2

6

3

7

4

8

Plant hyacinths and lilies
for a long-lasting display.

9	*12*
10	*13*
11	*14*

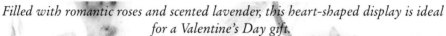

Filled with romantic roses and scented lavender, this heart-shaped display is ideal for a Valentine's Day gift.

1 Cut and shape a block of plastic foam for dried flowers to fit a heart-shaped box, and lightly mark the heart into quarters.

2 Fill one quarter with dried red rose heads, one with dried lavender, the third with dried poppy seedheads and the last with *Nigella orientalis*, massing the materials tightly to hide the foam.

15

16

17

18

19

20

21

22

23

24

25

26

An elegant table display
of candles and white lilies.

Salal tips, orange lilies, and marigolds make up this lovely domed arrangement in a reindeer moss-lined wire basket. The tulips will continue to grow and straighten in the soaked plastic foam and any lily buds will open, so allow for this in the display.

27

28

29

$\mathscr{M}$ARCH

But now
as March warms, and the rivulets
run like birdsong on the slopes,
and the branches of light sing in the hills,
slowly we return to earth

Wendell Berry

1

2

3

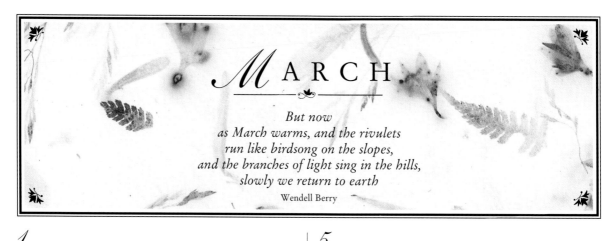

Scented hyacinths grow
well in bulb vases.

4

5

6

7

8

9

10

11

12

13

This beautiful wreath, suitable for Easter, is arranged in a soaked plastic foam ring using elaeagnus foliage, polyanthus plants and daffodils. Eight pieces of bark, and three raffia-wrapped blown eggs complete the festive design.

14	*17*
15	*18*
16	*19*

The explosion of new plant life in the spring is depicted in this arrangement of early flowers and foliage.

1 Line an urn with cellophane (plastic wrap) and wedge in a soaked plastic foam block. Pin reindeer moss around the rim using stub (floral) wires.

2 Arrange 15 pussy willow stems to establish the height and width of this symmetrical arrangement. Distribute 10 stems of white lilac throughout the pussy willow.

3 Position 15 pink cherry blossom stems throughout the display to reinforce the overall shape and complement the focal flower heads, the white lilac.

20

21

22

23

24

25

Delicate roses give this
wreath a spring-time feel.

26

27

28

29

30

31

$\mathcal{A}$ PRIL

This April, with his stormy showers
Doth make the earth yield pleasant flowers

Neve: Almanack, 1633

1

2

3

4

5

6

7

8

Mixed spring flowers are
used for this pedestal.

9

10

11

12

13

14

The simple beauty of an arrangement that relies entirely on one type of flower can be breathtaking.

1 Choose a basket in which a watertight container, such as a bucket, will fit. Fill the bucket with water then strip the lower leaves from 50 'Angelique' tulips.

2 Arrange the tulips in the bucket from the outside edge inwards, cutting the stems to form a shallow dome shape.

3 This arrangement will be viewed in the round so make sure you achieve a full, even dome.

15

16

This L-shaped design is
informal yet striking.

17

18

19

20

21

22

23

24

25

26

27

28

29

30

These massed flowers in bright colours are presented in a contemporary way but in pretty, old-fashioned terracotta thumb (rose) pots, the rustic charm of which has been enhanced by colouring their surfaces. Re-create this lovely arrangement using dried pink roses, sunflower heads, lavender, cinnamon sticks, *Craspedia globosa* and blue globe thistles, pushed into plastic foam for dried flowers. The display will have the greatest impact when used as a group but you could place the individual pots around the rooms of your house if you prefer.

$\mathcal{M}$ AY

In the last month of May
I made her posies;
I heard her often say
That she loved roses

Anon: Phillada Flouts Me

1

2

3

4

Rose tussie mussies make
lovely bride's bouquets.

5

6

7

8

This arrangement creates a colour collision between the pink phlox flower heads (these are 'Bright Eyes') and the vibrant reds of Virginia creeper. Arrange the phlox first and then weave the Virginia creeper through the phlox, to make a balanced display.

10

9

11

12	*15*
13	*16*
14	*17*

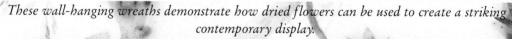

These wall-hanging wreaths demonstrate how dried flowers can be used to create a striking contemporary display.

1 For the red and yellow wreath, fix alternately coloured roses around the outside of a plastic foam ring for dried flowers by gluing their stems and pushing them into the foam. Leave a gap for the ribbon.

2 Continue building circles of roses, offsetting the colours against the last ring until the foam is covered. Attach a ribbon to hang the wreath. Use the same method for the globe thistle and white rose wreath.

18

19

20

21

22

23

24

25

This massed arrangement
has great visual impact.

26

27

28

29

30

31

JUNE

And what is so rare as a day in June?
Then, if ever, come perfect days;
Then heaven tries the earth if it be in tune
And over it softly her warm ear lays

J. R. Lowell: The Vision of Sir Lanfaul

1

2

3

4

5

6

7

8

This fruity swag will
brighten up any kitchen.

9	*12*
10	*13*
11	*14*

This shimmering bouquet would be perfect for a Golden Wedding celebration. It is hand spiralled for holding but can be unwrapped and placed straight into a vase of water.

1 Start the bouquet by hand spiralling alternate stems of golden yellow ranunculus and mimosa. (You will need about 20 stems of each.) Secure at the binding point with gold twine then trim the stems.

2 Wrap the bouquet in two shades of gold-coloured tissue paper, secure at the binding point and fan out. Finish off with a gold fabric bow and a dusting of gold glitter for extra sparkle.

15

16

Soft-looking goldenrod
offsets Peruvian lilies.

17

18

19

20

21

22

23

24

25

26

27

28

29

30

This delightful red rose ring can be hung on the wall or, with a candle at its centre, used as a table decoration for a romantic dinner for two. A bed of ivy leaves and bun moss, secured with stub (floral), wires is put on to a 15 cm (6 in) diameter plastic foam ring. It is then covered with 20 fresh rose heads. If you receive a bouquet of red roses, why not recycle them? After the rose blooms have fully blown open, cut down their stems for use in this circlet to extend their lives. Finally dehydrate the ring and continue to use it as a dried-flower display.

JULY

Then came hot July, boyling like to fire
That all his garments he had cast away

Edmund Spenser: The Faerie Queen

1

5

2

6

3

7

4

This pretty pitcher arrangement was hand spiralled using two bunches of sunny yellow sneezeweeds, 10 stems of 'Blue Butterfly' delphinium and three stems of dracaena. The beauty of hand spiralling is that once done the design can be place straight in a vase.

8

9

10

11

12

13

A garland of hydrangeas
looks lovely at a wedding.

14

15

16

17

18

19

Hang this swag in short loops at a table edge for the greatest impact. Short lengths of conifer, interspersed with pale pink roses, are bound to a rope with florist's wire. Loops at the rope ends allow it to be hung. For a summer Golden Wedding party, choose a combination of white and yellow roses; or for a wedding, reflect the choice of the blooms in the bride's bouquet. Keep the swags in a cool place until they are needed to preserve the flowers at their best for the guests to admire.

20

21

22

23

24

28

25

29

26

30

27

31

These beautiful, full-blown "antique" roses give an opulent, romantic feel to a very simple arrangement.

1 Place a watertight container in a terracotta flowerpot. Fill this and a pitcher with water.

2 Position the long-stemmed garden roses in the pitcher with the heads massed close together.

3 Mass the shorter open roses in a dome shape, in the flowerpot. Then place the containers together.

$\mathcal{A}$ UGUST

Fairest of months! Ripe summer's queen
The hay-day of the year
With robes that gleam with sunny sheen
Sweet August doth appear!

R. Combe Miller

1

2

3

4

Sweet summer blooms
make a romantic group.

5

6

7

8

9

10

11

12

13

This rich, predominantly pink and purple pot-pourri contains lavender, preserved (dried) apple slices, dried lemons, cloves, rose heads and buds, hibiscus buds and sea holly leaves. Several drops of pot-pourri essence are stirred in to create a lovely scent.

14

17

15

18

16

19

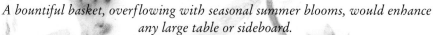

A bountiful basket, overflowing with seasonal summer blooms, would enhance any large table or sideboard.

1 Line a good-size basket with cellophane (plastic wrap) and trim the edges. Then secure two soaked plastic foam blocks in place using florist's adhesive tape.

2 Arrange 10 stems of *Viburnum tinus* in the foam to establish the shape then strengthen the outline with 15 stems of larkspur in different colours.

3 Place six lily stems (the ones used here are 'Stargazer') across one diagonal, some large ivy leaves around the lilies in the centre, and finish off with 10 stems of white phlox arranged across the opposite diagonal to the lilies.

20

21

22

23

24

25

Cottage-garden flowers
are arranged naturally.

26

27

28

29

30

31

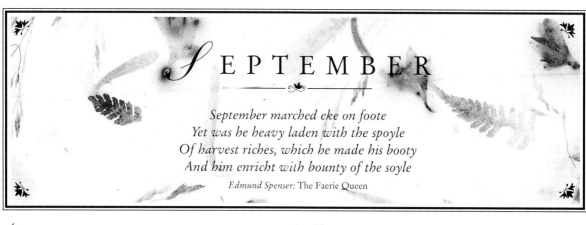

$\mathscr{S}$ EPTEMBER

September marched eke on foote
Yet was he heavy laden with the spoyle
Of harvest riches, which he made his booty
And him enricht with bounty of the soyle

Edmund Spenser: The Faerie Queen

1

2

3

4

5

6

7

8

A symbolic harvest swag
uses decorative grasses.

9

10

A tied sheaf of flowers is
arranged in the hand.

11

12

13

14

15

16

17

18

19

A heart of wheat, suitable for hanging in the kitchen,
celebrates the harvest and will last for years.
Small bundles of wheat ears are wired on to the heart
shape which is made of three lengths of
heavy-gauge garden wire.

20

21

22

23

24

25

This line arrangement
uses stunning amaryllis.

26

27

28

29

30

This lovely, seasonal display shows how colour can
be carried through a design. The apricot tone of the
spray roses, baby pumpkins and bird bath contrast
well with the red buds and yellow flowers of the
hypericum foliage.

O CTOBER

Seasons of mists and mellow fruitfulness,
Close bosom-friend of the maturing sun
Conspiring with him to load and bless
With fruit the vines that round the thatch-eaves run

John Keats: To Autumn

1

5

2

6

3

7

4

Fruit and flowers make
up this obelisk design.

8

This simple wooden trug containing autumn crocuses is a welcome sight as the year end approaches and most other plants are dying back. The bun moss and leaves give the design a lovely woodland feel, and a raffia bow provides a natural finishing touch.

9

10

11

12	*16*
13	*17*
14	*18*
15	*19*

This hand-spiralled wall-hanging sheaf would suit a country-style kitchen beautifully.

1 Hand spiral linseed, globe thistles, strawflowers, carthamus, and amaranthus.

2 Tie the completed sheaf with twine at the binding point.

3 If necessary, trim the stem ends. Finish off with a generous paper ribbon bow.

20

21

22

23

24

25

Striking colours make up
this Halloween display.

26

27

28

29

30

31

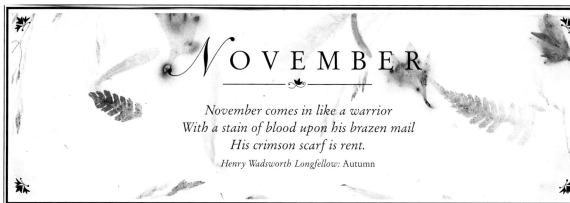

NOVEMBER

November comes in like a warrior
With a stain of blood upon his brazen mail
His crimson scarf is rent.

Henry Wadsworth Longfellow: Autumn

1

2

3

4

5

6

7

8

Exotic flowers can make a
spectacular display.

9

10

Fruit adds visual opulence
to this table display.

11

12

13

14

15

16

17

18

19

A humourous display that lifts the spirits as the
nights draw in, this pot would be a fun decoration
for a child's bedroom. Globe thistles, bleached cane
spirals and dried white roses are domed over an
edging of reindeer moss.

20

21

22

23

Dahlias with a seasonal
necklace of hazelnuts.

24

25

26

27

28

29

30

Miniature white cyclamen plants and pots of lily-of-
the-valley are arranged in a wire basket lined with
Spanish moss and finished off with paper ribbon
bows. The charm and purity of this long-lasting
display makes it an ideal gift for the birth of a baby.

DECEMBER

Over the woodlands brown and bare,
Over the harvest-fields forsaken,
Silent, and soft, and slow,
Descends the snow.

Henry Wadsworth Longfellow: Snowflakes

1

2

3

4

A candle-pot lantern is set
in a garland of twigs.

5

6

7

8

9

10

11

12

13

This Christmas candle pot uses the rich, dark seasonal colours to great effect. It includes red amaranthus, cones, magnolia leaves, holly oak, kutchi fruit, twigs, lavender, oranges, cinnamon sticks and mushrooms in a carefully balanced display.

14

15

Simple larch twigs create a
lovely festive wreath.

16

17

18

19

20

21

22

23

24

One hundred white tulip heads are used to achieve a
sophisticated purity in this Christmas wreath. Any
gaps in the soaked 25 cm (10 in) plastic foam ring are
infilled with holly, and a circle of holly encloses the
design, creating a dramatic contrast.

25

26

27

28

29

30

31

A dried-flower corsage can be used to embellish a
special Christmas gift. This one is made with a dried
pomegranate, fungi and double-leg mounted slices
of dried orange which are then bound together.
Raffia secures the decoration to the gift.